NOW YOU CAN READ....
THE BIRTH OF JESUS

STORY RETOLD BY ELAINE IFE

ILLUSTRATED BY ERIC ROWE

Published by Rourke Publications, Inc. P.O. Box 868, Windermere, Florida 32786. Copyright © 1983 by Rourke Publications, Inc. All copyrights reserved. No part of this book may be reproduced in any form without written permission from the publisher. Printed in the United States of America.

The Publishers acknowledge permission from Brimax Books for the use of the name "Now You Can Read" and "Large Type For First Readers" which identify Brimax Now You Can Read series.

Library of Congress Cataloging in Publication Data

Ife, Elaine, 1955-
 The brith of Jesus.

 (Now you can read—Bible stories)
 Summary: Recounts the various incidents surrounding the birth of Jesus from the Annunciation to the wise men's visit to the newborn babe.
 1. Jesus Christ—Nativity—Juvenile literature.
2. Bible stories, English—N.T. Matthew.
3. Bible stories, English—N.T. Luke. [1. Jesus Christ
—Nativity. 2. Bible stories—N.T. Matthew. 3. Bible stoires—N.T. Luke] I. Rowe, Eric, 1938- ill.
II. Title. III. Series.
BT315.2.I37 1983   226'.09505   83-13808
ISBN 0-86625-216-9

Ife

GROLIER ENTERPRISES CORP.

NOW YOU CAN READ....
THE BIRTH OF JESUS

5824

Long ago, in a small town called
Nazareth, there lived a girl named
Mary. At that time, many men had
forgotten about God. He decided to
send a little child to live and
grow up among the people. This
little child would teach them about
God.

God knew that Mary loved Him, so He chose her to be the mother of His child. He sent an angel called Gabriel to tell Mary about the Baby. Mary was alone in her house when she saw the angel standing beside her. She was afraid and hid her eyes.

The angel looked kindly at Mary and said, "Do not be afraid, Mary. God has sent me to tell you good news. Soon you will have a baby. It will be a boy and His name will be Jesus. He will be a holy child, for He will be the Son of God."

In the same town, a carpenter called
Joseph lived. He wanted to take
care of Mary and the Baby because
he loved her. Joseph took Mary
to be his wife.

The king of the land wanted all the people to be counted, so Mary and Joseph had to go back to the place where they were born.

It was a long way to go, so they had a little donkey for Mary to ride while Joseph walked by her side. At last, they came to an inn.

They were very tired
and needed a rest.
Joseph knocked at
the door. The door
opened and the
innkeeper said,
"What do you
want?"
"Have you a bed
for the night,
please?" asked
Joseph. "My wife
is very tired, for
we have come a
long way."

"I am very sorry," said the innkeeper, shaking his head. "There is no room for you here. If you would like to stay in the stable with the animals, you are welcome to rest there. It is warm and dry." "Thank you," said Joseph. "That will do very well."

They followed the innkeeper to the stable, and there in the night, the Baby Jesus was born.

There was nothing for the Baby to wear. Mary wrapped Him in strips of cloth. There was nowhere for the Baby to sleep. Joseph made Him a little bed in the place where food for the cows and donkeys was kept. It was called a manger. He put warm, dry straw in it and Mary laid the Baby there to sleep.

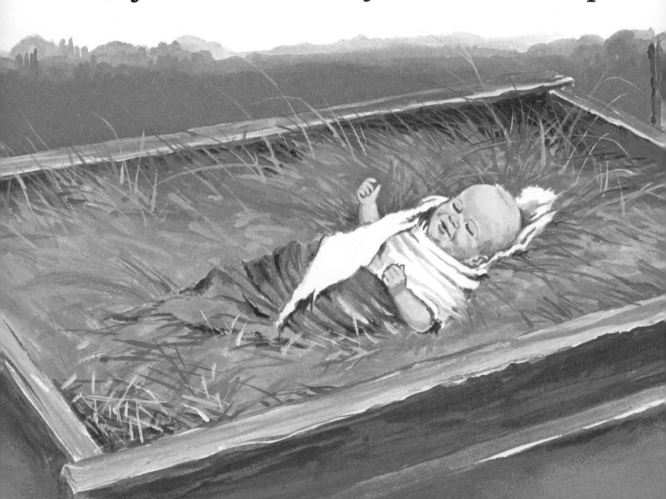

Outside, the night was dark and cold. In the fields close to the town, some shepherds were looking after their sheep. They sat close to the fire, warming their hands and talking to each other.

Suddenly, a great light shone in the sky and an angel stood in front of them.

They were all afraid but the angel said,

"Do not be afraid, for I have come to tell you good news. Tonight, the Lord Jesus has been born. Go to Him. Follow the bright star in the sky and it will lead you to the stable where He lies."

Then the sky was filled with angels who sang,

"Glory to God in Heaven
Peace on Earth
And Joy to all Men."

At once the shepherds set off, following a bright star in the sky which led them to the place where Jesus lay. With them they took their sheep in case a wolf should attack them.

The shepherds knocked
at the stable door
and Joseph let them
in.

They knelt down
beside the Baby
because they knew
He was very special.

Mary did not know why anyone should come to see her baby, but she said nothing.
Then the shepherds left the stable and went into the town to let everyone know about Jesus.

Three wise men from the East had been keeping watch on the stars in the sky. They knew that a great king was to be born. They were waiting for a sign to show where to find Him.

At last, a bright star showed them the way.

They rode across many lands following
the star. They thought they would
find Him in a palace, but the star
led them to a poor stable. They
left their camels outside and going
in, found Jesus lying in a manger.

At once they knew that He was the
one they had been seeking.

Each wise man had brought a present
for Jesus which was laid down
beside Him.

When they had gone, Mary thought again for a long time. Why had the shepherds and the wise men come so far to see her baby? Then she picked up Jesus and held Him close to her, thinking about what the angel had said.

All these appear in the pages of the story. Can you find them?

Mary

angel

Joseph

donkey

innkeeper

Jesus

manger

star

shepherds

wise men

Now tell the story in your own words.